GREAT COMEBACK CHAMPIONS

Arthur ASHE
Tennis Legend

Written and Illustrated by Jim Spence

THE ROURKE PRESS, INC.
VERO BEACH, FL 32964

© 1995 The Rourke Press, Inc.

All rights reserved. No part of this book may be reproduced or utilized in any form or by any means, electronic or mechanical including photocopying, recording or by any information storage and retrieval system without permission in writing from the publisher.

Edited by Sandra A. Robinson and Pamela J.P. Schroeder

LIBRARY OF CONGRESS CATALOGING-IN-PUBLICATION DATA

Spence, Jim
    Arthur Ashe, tennis legend / written and illustrated by Jim Spence.
       p. cm. — (Great comeback champions)
    Summary: Describes the series of triumphs of this Afro-American tennis player and shows how he was a winner both on and off the court.
    ISBN 1-57103-004-2
    1. Ashe, Arthur—Juvenile literature. 2. Tennis players—United States—Biography—Juvenile literature. [1. Ashe, Arthur. 2. Tennis players. 3. Afro-Americans—Biography.] I. Title II. Series: Spence, Jim. Great comeback champions.
GV994.A7S64   1995
796.342'092—dc20
[B]   95-5361
                                                                                               CIP
                                                                                                      AC

Printed in the USA

The huge crowd leans forward for the most important point of the match. The server tosses the ball high in the air and smashes it onto his opponent's court, for the game-winning point. "Game, set and match," calls the announcer. "Ladies and gentlemen, your new Wimbledon Champion—Arthur Ashe!"

Starting Out

Arthur Ashe grew up near Brookfield Park, Virginia. His father was caretaker there. The park had a big swimming pool, basketball courts and tennis courts, too. Brookfield Park was where young Arthur learned to play the game of tennis.

Arthur's mother loved him very much. She wanted to help him grow up to be someone special. Even before he was in school, Arthur's mother taught him how to read and write.

By the time he was only 10 years old, Arthur Ashe's tennis skills were something to watch. Ronald Charity, a tennis teacher, helped Arthur improve his game. Later Mr. Charity introduced him to Dr. Robert Johnson of Lynchburg, Virginia.

Dr. Johnson was known for coaching the great Althea Gibson, the first black tennis player to win England's Wimbledon tournament.

Dr. Johnson taught Arthur the importance of good behavior on and off the tennis courts. Arthur learned he was not only representing his sport, but his race as well.

Going to College

In 1961, Arthur took a scholarship to play tennis for the University of California at Los Angeles (UCLA). He was the first African-American student to be offered a scholarship with UCLA. At college, he met Pancho Gonzales—a top tennis player. Pancho helped Arthur develop a strong serve-and-volley game.

In 1965, Arthur Ashe became the best college player in the nation when he won the National Collegiate Athletic Association (NCAA) singles and doubles titles.

Living His Dreams

At UCLA, Arthur dreamed of someday playing for America's Davis Cup Team. In Davis Cup competition, nations would match teams of their best players against other nations' players. The Davis Cup winner is the world's number one team.

In 1963, Arthur's dream came true when he was the first black player named to America's Davis Cup Team.

Arthur was honored to play for his country. From 1963 to 1978 he set a Davis Cup record of 27 victories and only five losses.

Later in his career, he was named Captain of the Davis Cup Team. In 1981 and 1982, America won the Davis Cup under the leadership of Arthur Ashe.

In 1968, in Forest Hills, New York, Arthur Ashe entered America's biggest tournament—the U.S. Open. Arthur met Tom Okker of the Netherlands in the finals. He played a great match and won! Arthur had truly become one of America's finest players.

His father knew how hard Arthur worked to be a good player, and a good person, too. As Arthur held the winning trophy, his father felt such pride that tears ran down his cheeks.

After he won the U.S. Open, Arthur was ranked among the top players in the world. In 1975, he reached the finals at Wimbledon, the world's most historic tennis tournament. Arthur faced the number one player in the world—Jimmy Connors.

No one thought Arthur could win—Connors was too powerful a player. However, Arthur wisely changed his style of play by hitting low, soft shots—shots that Connors didn't expect. Arthur Ashe stunned the world by winning the Wimbledon championship in four straight sets.

Fighting Back

Soon after winning Wimbledon, Arthur began to have eye problems, and also had to have surgery on his heel. His world ranking in tennis fell to number 257. Arthur had already had a great career in tennis. It would have been easy for him to retire. When Arthur decided to try playing again, his wife and many other people supported him.

Arthur worked his way back to number seven in the world, and won Comeback Player of the Year in 1978.

Reaching Out

At the age of 36, Arthur Ashe suffered a heart attack that ended his tennis career. He began to use his talents to teach tennis to less fortunate children. He became a television commentator and wrote several books. Arthur also traveled the world to speak out against discrimination, in support of human rights.

In 1988, Arthur found out he had the fatal disease called AIDS. Doctors believed he got AIDS through an infected blood transfusion when he had his heart operation. To help educate people about this disease, he founded the Arthur Ashe Foundation for the Defeat of AIDS.

On February 7, 1993, Arthur Ashe passed away. "Arthur Ashe touched many people by the way he lived his life. He was a true crusader for human rights and his life's work, courage and spirit will live forever," believes longtime tennis great, Billie Jean King.

GREAT COMEBACK CHAMPIONS

Arthur ASHE

TIMELINE AND TRIUMPHS

1943   Born July 10 in Richmond, Virginia

1960-61   Won National Junior Indoor Title

1963   First black player named to American Davis Cup Team

1963-78   Set Davis Cup record—27 victories, five losses

1965   Won National Collegiate Athletic Association Championship (singles and doubles)

1967   U.S. Clay Court Champion

1968   U.S. National Champion

1968   U.S. Open Champion

1970   Australian Open Champion

1971 French Open Doubles Champion

1975 U.S. Clay Court Champion

1975 Wimbledon Champion

1981 Davis Cup Team Captain

1985 Davis Cup Team Captain

1985 Voted into International Tennis Hall of Fame

1993 Passed away, February 7

GREAT COMEBACK CHAMPIONS

ARTHUR ASHE
Tennis Legend

BO JACKSON
Super Athlete

JOE MONTANA
The Comeback Kid

JULIE KRONE
Fearless Jockey

MUHAMMAD ALI
The Greatest

NANCY KERRIGAN
Courageous Skater